Made in the USA
Monee, IL
30 July 2021

74611292R00063